THE
GHOSTLY TALES
OF
SAVANNAH

Published by Arcadia Children's Books
An imprint of Arcadia Publishing
Charleston, SC
www.arcadiapublishing.com

Spooky America is a trademark of Arcadia Publishing, Inc.

First published 2020

Manufactured in the United States

ISBN 978-1-4671-9807-3

Library of Congress Control Number: 2020938910

Notice: The information in this book is true and complete to the best of our knowledge. It is offered without guarantee on the part of the author or Arcadia Publishing. The author and Arcadia Publishing disclaim all liability in connection with the use of this book.

Photo credits: used throughout Eugenia Petrovskaya/Shutterstock.com, Nataliia K/Shutterstock.com, In-Finity/Shutterstock.com, vectorkuro/Shutterstock.com; p. iv-v netsign33/Shutterstock.com; the Hornbills Studio/Shutterstock.com; Caso Alfonso/Shutterstock.com, Ivakoleva/Shutterstock.com, LDDesign/Shutterstock.com; p. vi, 40, 86 zef art/Shutterstock.com; p. 4, 46, 92 Joe Techapanupreeda/Shutterstock.com; p. 9, 110 Ihnatovich Maryia/Shutterstock.com; p. 12, 52, 98 andreiuc88/Shutterstock.com; p. 16–17 Pavel Kovaricek/Shutterstock.com; p. 20, 58, 108 Stephen B. Goodwin/Shutterstock.com; p. 26, 66 Solid photos/Shutterstock.com; p. 32, 74 AbzofSteel/Shutterstock.com; p. 37 KsanaGraphica/Shutterstock.com; p. 57 Forgem/Shutterstock.com; p. 63 Cattallina/Shutterstock.com; p. 70 Stock2You/Shutterstock.com; p. 96-97 Alex Tihonovs/Shutterstock.com.

Spooky America

THE
GHOSTLY TALES
OF
SAVANNAH

JESSA DEAN

Adapted from *Historic Haunts of Savannah*, by Michael Harris and Linda Sickler

ARCADIA
PUBLISHING

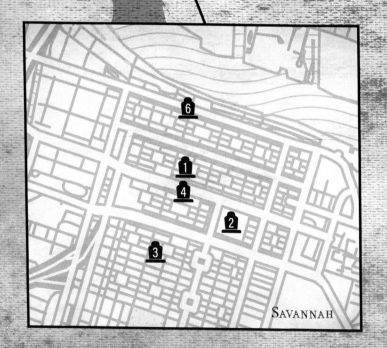

NORTH CAROLINA

ATLANTA
5

SOUTH
CAROLINA

GEORGIA

ALABAMA

ATLANTIC OCEAN

FLORIDA

6

1

4

2

3

SAVANNAH

Table of Contents & Map Key

Land of the Living and the Dead

What if I told you that there was a city, maybe not far from you, where ghosts walked beside the living? Where ghouls hid in the shadows and legends were real? If you like feeling a shiver down your spine, read on! The haunted history of Savannah doesn't care if you believe in ghosts or not, but even the most skeptical reader can't ignore the overwhelming proof of the supernatural that lurks around every corner.

Savannah is on the coast of Georgia, right on the Atlantic Ocean. It has been a busy seaport since the early days of the United States. People from all over the world come to Savannah to tour its historic homes, wander under trees dripping with Spanish moss, and enjoy its beautiful squares, with flowers and fountains always on display. But just as many people, if not more, come to be scared. Who would think that such a beautiful town had so many spooky, creepy stories that would have you sleeping with the lights on?

It's said that there's a ghost story for every building in Savannah. Haunted tours take visitors through the streets every day. Braver souls wait until after dark, when the shadows play tricks on you. Maybe you'll see something that will scare you so much, you'll pee in your pants! It just may be the most haunted city in

America, which is why it's the best city if you like to be scared.

The dead—and the undead—have made Savannah their playground. Within this book, you'll hear tales of murder, curses, zombies, and more. You'll learn about the origins of superstitions and rituals that make sure the dead stay dead. But are the tales really true? Can one place be *that* haunted?

Let's take a walk through Savannah and see for ourselves. What's the worst that could happen?

CHAPTER 1

Savannah's First Execution

Not long after British settlers landed in Savannah in 1733, a woman named Alice Riley arrived from Ireland. She came to America in search of a better life, like so many people did and still do. You know about slaves brought to the United States against their will, but other people freely made the decision to come here and work as a servant. They signed contracts to work for a period of time so they could repay their master for the trip across the ocean.

Alice was supposed to land in Philadelphia, a popular destination for immigrants from Ireland. But crossing the Atlantic Ocean was dangerous, even under the best conditions. A winter storm hit Alice's ship. Between illness and lack of food and clean water, most of the people on board died. Can you imagine? Dead bodies lining the hull of the ship, rotting away under your feet and stinking up the place? The boat rocking so much you barfed over the side? Meanwhile, the only food was scraps that hadn't washed overboard.

It's amazing Alice made it out alive. She was one of only forty passengers—six women and thirty-four men—who were rescued and taken to Savannah. Georgia was still a colony at the time. The rules of the Georgia colony discouraged servants, but James Oglethorpe, the founder of Savannah, took pity on the survivors. He purchased them and sent them to work for various people in the colony. Some of them worked for lonely widows who needed help, but not Alice.

History tells us that Alice's master was NOT a good guy. He treated his servants really badly. He was very ill, and it was Alice's job to keep him clean. She had to comb lice out of his hair. Even worse, she had to pick food out of his greasy beard. And still, he was an awful person. She must have been so grossed out, but she couldn't do anything. He was her master.

Finally, Alice and another servant, Richard White, decided they'd had enough and weren't going to be treated badly anymore. They took their revenge against their master, first by strangling him and then, to make sure he was dead, by holding his head underwater. They ran, but eventually, they were caught and found guilty of murder, the first in Savannah. They were both sentenced to death by hanging. Alice was pregnant and pleaded for mercy, so the executions were delayed. But after the baby was born, the date for her execution was set: January 19, 1735.

A platform was set up in Percival Square under an old oak tree to carry out Alice's sentence by hanging. Percival Square also held the city's courthouse and jail. The gallows became a permanent feature for years, and many people were hanged for their crimes. The public came out to watch the gruesome sight of bodies hanging from the tree, eyes bulging and face twisting as they gasped for air. Percival Square is called Wright Square now. It's one of the city's most beautiful squares, despite its brutal history.

Alice's story is particularly famous. She was the first person executed in not only Savannah, but also in all of the Georgia colony. The crowd came to see a show, and Alice gave them one. She screamed and cursed until she finally choked to death. She even cursed the tree that held the noose that went around her neck. The executioner supposedly left her hanging there for three days.

If you visit Wright Square, make sure to look

at the northeast corner closely. Spanish moss grows on basically every tree in Savannah, but not on the ones in that corner, thanks to Alice's curse. You'll have to imagine the gallows if you visit, but if you're lucky, you might just spot Alice.

Yes. You heard me right. Multiple sightings of Alice have occurred since her hanging. Late at night, she can sometimes be found wandering the square, crying out. Every year, the police department gets several calls of a wild-eyed woman roaming around, searching desperately for her baby. What would you do if you saw her?

Her partner-in-crime, Richard, was hanged later. Only, according to legend, it didn't work. The sentence was to be hanged until he died, but Richard just wouldn't die. So they hanged him again the next day. And again the day after that. Was Richard just stubborn? Did the executioner do something wrong? Or was Richard a zombie, part of the undead? Only the gravedigger knows the truth.

Death Rituals

Savannah is full of the strange and unusual, especially when it comes to beliefs around death. Some of the strangest customs surrounding death come from the Victorian era, which was from about 1840 to about 1900 (named for England's Queen Victoria, who was on the throne at this time). Death became something of a fascination for the people who lived back then. This was partly due to the influence of

Queen Victoria mourning the sudden death of her young husband in 1861.

Victoria was so devastated that she never really recovered. For the rest of her life—forty years—she wore black to mourn him. This carried over into the way the public dressed; black had not been a popular color before then. Now you'd never know that, since black clothes are everywhere. Who knew a queen would be such a fashion icon?

But the queen wasn't the only influence on the Victorians and their obsession with death. At the time, only one in four children lived to adulthood. Illness and death were always present. And because many of the settlers of Savannah were British, their beliefs crossed the ocean.

When someone died, Victorians had elaborate rituals. They stopped all the clocks in the house, as if to freeze time at the moment of death. They pulled the curtains shut and covered all the mirrors, believing that this would keep their loved one's spirit from getting trapped in the reflective surface. Special wreaths with black ribbons were hung on the door to alert the neighbors that death had arrived.

For three or four days, people watched over the body constantly, not leaving it alone for a minute. This "wake," as it was called, was partly to let family and friends say goodbye but also to make sure that the person was really dead. Seriously. Back then, medical science wasn't nearly what it is today. They couldn't always be 100 percent sure the person was dead. What if they had just fallen into a coma and were buried alive? I don't know about you, but being buried alive is my worst nightmare.

Today, funeral homes prepare the body for a wake or funeral with all kinds of chemicals and makeup. They preserve the body with a liquid called embalming fluid, so it doesn't rot and stink. You can kind of think of it like taking a cucumber and turning it into a pickle. A cucumber goes bad in a few days if you don't eat it, but if you seal it up in a jar with vinegar and spices, it lasts a long time. Embalming fluid kind of does the same thing but from the inside. It keeps the body from smelling and decomposing long enough to have a funeral.

But back in Victorian times, embalming wasn't very common. Victorians had to use flowers and candles to cover up the smell of the dead body.

When the wake was over, the body would be taken out feet first so that the person couldn't look back into the house. This was so the person's spirit wouldn't remain in the house, or, even worse, take someone else with them when they left. In fact, many Victorians were so worried about being possessed by the dead person's spirit that they turned over or removed photographs of living family members just in case.

Death was such a part of their lives that many Victorians even made adjustments to their houses. It seems weird to us now, but their superstitions guided their behavior. Some houses had a special "coffin corner" cut into the stairwell. Since the entryways were so small,

the cut gave a little extra room to get a coffin out of the front door. Some people even went to the extreme of building a display window at the front of the house to hold a coffin. That way, people passing by the house could pay their respects to the dead.

Irish settlers in Savannah had certain customs of their own during a wake. Instead of covering the windows when someone died, they opened them wide. Women gathered to perform a ritual of washing and dressing the body. Sometimes, Irish wakes turned into rowdy parties. They even pulled the body out of the casket so the deceased could have one last dance. Just picture it: people dancing around the room and propping up a dead body, moving its legs and arms. But even though they got close to the body, the Irish still had the same worries about being possessed. Everyone wore black, believing it made them appear to be shadows so the spirit of the dead wouldn't enter them.

Children's funerals and wakes were the exceptions to wearing black. Children who had died were often dressed in white. Women also dressed in white with white veils and would carry the child in a white coffin. They would also carry white ostrich plumes.

These traditions and superstitions may seem weird or super old-fashioned, but if you've ever been to a funeral, you can see how some of them have continued. Most cultures have rituals and beliefs surrounding death. Different families may even have their own, passed down through generations. Are the superstitions silly? Maybe. But it's probably a good idea to follow them anyway. You never know; they may be the only things keeping the dead from becoming undead.

The Frankenstein
of Savannah

So what roams the dark streets of Savannah? Ghosts? Zombies? Mythical creatures? All of the above? What would you do if you encountered something you couldn't explain? Would you run the other way or face it head-on and attack?

Most people try to avoid things that scare them or things they can't explain. But in the early 1800s, some residents of one of the poorest neighborhoods in Savannah decided to confront someone that scared them, and it ended badly. At least, that's what the legends say.

There are many versions of the story of the so-called "Frankenstein of Savannah," Rene Rhondolia. Depending on who tells the tale, he was either a child who looked like a man or a man who had the brain of a child. There are even different versions of his name in the various stories. But one thing that everyone agrees on is that he was more man than child in his appearance, even at a young age. They say he stood seven feet tall and weighed five hundred pounds, with hands as big as hens! Can you imagine how scary he must have seemed standing at the end of a dark street, towering over anyone who came close?

Rene didn't know his own strength, and he ended up hurting small animals when he tried to play with them. Tales of what happened next vary in some of the details, but the story is basically the same no matter who tells it.

Rene lived in a neighborhood called Foley's Alley, which was full of poor Irish immigrants. When the neighbors found out about Rene accidentally killing animals, a group of them made Rene's parents lock him up. Their house backed up to an old cemetery, and Rene's dad put spikes on the wall so Rene couldn't climb over it and escape. His parents tried to keep him safe, but in the end, they couldn't protect him from people who couldn't—or didn't want to—understand.

One night, a child was found murdered in the street, with its neck broken. Locals immediately blamed Rene. There was no investigation or team of people at the crime scene like you see on television. A mob of angry and scared neighbors went straight to

Rene's house instead. Rene's mother begged them to leave her boy alone, but they dragged him away. He fought back, but ultimately, they hanged him until he died.

It seems like the story should have ended there, but then again, this is Savannah.

The mob thought they took care of the killer, but then another child's body showed up at Colonial Park Cemetery, the cemetery near Rene's house. Other children disappeared from the neighborhood. People began to whisper about Rene having come back from the dead. They told tales of Rene's ghost haunting Foley's Alley and lurking in the cemetery.

Every time someone told the story of Rene Rhondolia, it changed slightly. Some told tales of city officials caging him and parading him around like a circus sideshow. Or that a mob followed a trail of dead animals to capture him and hang him in the woods. Or that hair covered him from head to toe, like a wolf man.

So what's the real story? Who was Rene? No one knows. There are no records of Rene. No one can verify that he actually existed. You've probably seen those television shows that investigate paranormal activity and tales. They've done stories on Rene, of course. But whenever someone does a story, they never give proof that he existed. No newspaper articles, public records, or anything official have provided actual evidence of Rene or his family. It seems he came straight out of people's imaginations.

What do you think? Was Rene an actual person or just a bedtime story to scare kids into behaving? Better not take any chances going down dark alleys just in case.

CHAPTER 4

Very Superstitious

We've talked about some of the Victorian superstitions that surrounded the wake and preparation for burial, but there are many more that made their way into Savannah's society. You've probably read myths and legends where things happening in nature were thought to be because of the gods. For example, if it didn't rain and all the crops died, it was because the gods were angry—things like that. Well, the

Victorians had similar beliefs when it came to nature and death.

Rain could be positive or negative, depending on the situation. Rain falling while carrying a coffin to the grave meant the deceased would go to Heaven. If a thunderclap happened right after the body had been buried, they believed the deceased had reached the pearly gates. On the other hand, rain in an open grave meant a close family member of the deceased would die. Large raindrops during a storm were a signal that someone had just died.

Victorians also believed that flowers had specific meanings. So it's no surprise that flowers played a role in Victorian beliefs about death. People at this time even used flowers to communicate with each other, a practice known as floriography.

Victorian society had rules to follow, which meant people often couldn't say what they meant. Flowers became a way to send coded messages to people. You could share a deep secret with someone or tell them you loved them. Flower dictionaries became hugely popular as people searched for ways to express their emotions. For example, violets indicated devotion and loyalty, but lavender meant you weren't trusted.

If someone had lived a good life, the Victorians believed that flowers would grow on top of their grave. For people who were less worthy, they believed only weeds would grow.

Flowers could also be premonitions of death or signs of the supernatural. If your garden held one snowdrop flower, it could mean death. You also had to make sure to never put red and white flowers together in a vase without another color, especially in a hospital. Doing so meant death was on the way.

The scent of flowers was equally powerful

to the Victorians. Noticing the scent of roses when there weren't any roses around meant someone was going to die soon. Smell someone's favorite floral perfume after they'd died? It meant their ghost was watching nearby.

Even animals held superstition and symbolism for the Victorians. If you saw a bird doing specific things, it could mean death was coming. Birds pecking on the window or crashing into it meant someone had died, as did a sparrow landing on your piano. (I have no idea how a sparrow would get into your house.) Hearing the call of birds like curlews and owls foretold a death. There's even a nursery rhyme about what it means to see a certain number of magpies. It wasn't just birds, though. If your dog howled while someone lay sick in bed, death was certain. Death was also on the way if a firefly, or lightning bug, appeared in your house.

Animals belonging to the household were protected, though. If many members of a family had died, the Victorians tied black ribbons around every living thing that entered the house. They believed this would keep dogs, chickens, and other animals from harm.

These are just some of the things Victorians believed. Lots seem to predict death, and others may seem ridiculous. But think about what superstitions we have today: people don't like to walk under ladders (bad luck), they hold their breath when they drive past a graveyard, or they throw salt over their shoulder if they spill it. Superstitions are often passed down from our families and our different cultures.

What about you? Do you have any superstitions? Do you believe they protect you?

Paranormal Activity

If you watch any paranormal investigation shows, you've seen stories from Savannah. It's a popular place for these shows to visit because of how much activity surrounds the town. With the dead walking freely among the living in Savannah, there's plenty of material for ambitious TV hosts!

Savannah's old homes are a draw for tourists, with mansions full of beautiful antiques, architecture, and historical tales. But many of these homes also hold stories of murder, revenge, and heartbreak. And many have restless spirits who can't—or won't—leave.

One of the most popular places to try to capture all things paranormal is the Sorrel-Weed House. Using ultraviolet light, paranormal experts have seen handprints all over the basement—handprints of the dead. Visitors have also seen a clothes hanger move completely on its own upstairs. And if you go out to the carriage house, you just might hear the voice of a long-dead slave.

So why is there so much paranormal activity in this particular house? Some say it's because two violent deaths happened here.

Francis Sorrel began building the house in 1835 and lived there with his wife Matilda and their children and servants after its completion in 1840. Francis was a very successful businessman in Savannah, and Matilda came from a wealthy family whose money helped Francis make his own fortune. The Sorrel-Weed House was known for hosting fabulous parties, with all the important people in Savannah attending, dressed in their finest clothes.

One night, the household was busy preparing for a party when Matilda because upset at her husband and one of the slaves, Molly. Matilda ran from the carriage house to the second floor of the main house. Before anyone could stop her, Matilda dove off the balcony and landed in the courtyard below with a splat. Her body lay twisted atop blood-covered stones where guests usually danced and laughed the night away. It was a horrible tragedy. But is that the whole story? Some witnesses said that Matilda didn't jump but fell off the balcony. There's also a dispute over whether she fell from the second or third story. Regardless, the outcome was the same.

Legend says that the household staff was furious. Matilda was beloved and had been very fragile emotionally. They thought Francis and Molly drove Matilda to jump, and since the staff couldn't go against their master, they took it out on Molly.

Shortly after Matilda's funeral, the staff burst into the room where Molly slept and hanged her from the beams in the ceiling. It's said that Francis stood by and watched without interfering. But that's only one version of the story. Some say that members of Matilda's family killed Molly. Others say Molly hanged herself. There's no official record of Molly's death, but sadly, that wasn't unusual for slaves.

If you listen carefully while walking the grounds of the Sorrel-Weed House, you might hear Molly begging for help. Ghost hunters have recorded a woman's voice saying, "Help! Oh, Francis, help! Oh my God! Oh my God!" You might also see Matilda wandering the courtyard wearing Victorian-era clothes. Their presence can turn even skeptics into believers.

But Matilda and Molly aren't the only dead

who walk the courtyard and hallways of the Sorrel-Weed House. Visitors to the house have often seen a woman dressed in black in the basement and courtyard, sometimes glaring back at them for disturbing her. Some have even captured photographs of the woman in black and a man with a black mustache dressed in clothes from the 1800s. There's photographic evidence of a little girl in the drawing room who can't be identified and also of a man who might have been a soldier. Nobody knows who he was.

Like many buildings in Savannah's historic district, the Sorrel-Weed House was built on top of a bloody, Revolutionary War battlefield. The Siege of Savannah took place there in October 1779. As workers began foundation work for the house in 1835, they found the bones of soldiers who had been buried where they died on the battlefield.

Seems like a bad idea to disturb the dead, don't you think? Would you want to live in a house knowing it was built on top of a graveyard? And is the battlefield the reason for so many paranormal encounters in the mansion? Who knows? But if you visit, make sure you keep your camera handy to capture a ghost or two.

Rules for Mourning

In addition to their superstitions surrounding the dead, Victorian-era society had strict rules for remembering the dead. It probably doesn't surprise you that only the wealthy people of Savannah could afford the elaborate rituals surrounding death. People without money had to work instead of watching the body every minute. They couldn't afford fancy coffins and windows where the public could pay their respects. But they were still expected to follow the mourning customs or risk being cast out by their community.

Queen Victoria wore black for forty years to mourn, which was a little extreme. But still, the rules of the time forced women who lost their husbands to wear black for a year and a half. If you couldn't afford to buy new black clothes, you had to dye your other clothes black. You also had to purchase stationery and handkerchiefs with black borders on them to make sure everyone knew your husband had died. The more recent the death, the wider the border.

After the year-and-a-half, a widow could go into "half-mourning." She could add a small amount of grey or white to her wardrobe. Maybe even a little jewelry, as long as it was an approved stone that was, of course, black. She could also wear different types of fabric that made the black shine a little. Once she hit the two-year mark, she could finally start adding colors back to her clothing. Children also had rules on how they dressed in mourning. They wore white trimmed with black or grey. Even their dolls were dressed to match. They didn't have to follow the rules for a full two years, though. Six months was long enough for children who had lost their parents or siblings.

Once photograph technology became widely available, the Victorians changed the way they celebrated and remembered their dead. Once someone died, families would often hire a photographer to come to the house to take photographs that could be shared with loved ones. Some were of the dead person in the coffin, but others were made to be as life-like as possible. Really. The dead person's cheeks were painted rosy so they would look alive. The family would open the eyelids, or paint eyes on top of the eyelids if necessary, all so the photos could look more realistic—or at least like the dead person was alive. (Even if they did look kind of creepy.) They even used props to hold the dead body upright so the deceased could "interact" with the family in the photos like the Irish did at their wakes. (Can you imagine families doing that today?)

It wasn't just photographs that Victorians used to remember the dead. They often took hair from the deceased to make jewelry. This was especially popular in the second stage of mourning. Bracelets, rings, belt buckles, and other items held either pieces or full strands of hair. If a loved one didn't want a piece of jewelry as a memento, they could always have a sculpture made with different shades of the deceased's hair. It may sound strange or gross to us now, but since hair doesn't decay easily, it was a way for the Victorians to keep their loved ones close after death. (If you ask your parents, they may actually have a snippet of your hair from when you were a baby. So maybe the hair thing isn't so weird. Or maybe it is?)

But tell me, was it a good idea for the living to mess with the dead like this? If you watch horror movies, you know that it doesn't always turn out well when a vengeful ghost is involved. It's probably a good idea to leave the bodies alone and let them rest in peace.

The Lovely Ghost

It's not often that you hear about friendly ghosts, is it? You may have watched them on cartoons or movies, but the stories told around campfires and on late-night walks are always scary. Savannah has more than its share of monsters under the beds, but it also has a famous ghost love story. Now before you get all grossed out or giggly about it, you should know that it involves the family of someone you might have heard of—especially if you were ever a Girl Scout.

Every Girl Scout knows that Juliette Gordon Low founded the Girl Scouts organization. She did so right in the heart of Savannah. You can even visit the house where she lived, which thousands of Girl Scouts do every year. But Juliette's parents, William W. ("Willie") and Nellie Gordon, are famous more for their deaths than their lives.

The story goes that Nellie and Willie met in 1853 at a party at Yale University's Law Library. Nellie came sliding down the railing of the staircase and crashed into Willie. She crushed his brand-new hat but stole his heart. He told people that right then and there, he knew he'd marry her, and they did get married. They had many wonderful years together before Willie died in 1912. Nellie was heartbroken. She grieved for Willie and never remarried.

But Willie was waiting for her too. Five years later, Nellie was dying. Willie showed up at their home, dressed in his best grey suit, and went up to Nellie's room. Their daughter-in-law and butler both saw Willie exit Nellie's room and head down the stairs toward the front door of the house. Can you imagine how weird that must have been to see Willie walking around like he'd never died?

Just before Willie showed up, Nellie had told her family not to mourn her, that she would be back with her husband. She lapsed into a coma, but just before Willie was spotted on the stairs leaving her room, Nellie's eyes flew open wide. She sat straight up in bed, and her face lit up. She reached out as if to touch someone, and then she peacefully died.

Like most ghost stories in Savannah, the line between reality and legend is a blurry one, even when it comes to true love. Did Willie really come to take Nellie with him? Was it to make her transition to the afterlife easier? Or was it all just wishful thinking by the family? The only thing we know for sure is that Willie and Nellie loved each other very much. And the power of that love story has kept this tale alive for generations.

The house, now known as the Juliette Gordon Low Birthplace, is no stranger to other ghost encounters as well. The staff who manage the home for the Girl Scouts have reported all kinds of ghostly visitations over the years. People report seeing Nellie or Willie's mother walking in the garden behind the house. Various ghostly figures are seen in the hallways and on the stairs. And you better watch your electronic devices when you're in the house. Apparently, the ghosts are fascinated by them. Staff will often enter the house in the morning to find the ghosts have turned on equipment and printed pages all night.

Now that's the kind of ghost I can deal with.

Them Bones

With all the dead buried in Savannah, it's no surprise that the city has ALSO had an obsession with bones throughout the years. (Lots of obsessions in Savannah.) But even our earliest ancestors had a fascination with bones. Only, they were usually associated with life, not death. It's only in modern times that we've come to think of bones as creepy or scary. Isn't it weird how you give a dog an animal bone to chew on, but if you saw that same bone in a field, the hair on the back of your neck would rise?

In the past, bones were thought to be magical, holding mystical power. Skulls, vertebrae, and shoulder blades were considered the most powerful for use in rituals. Some believed bones could even be used to create a person or bring one back to life. People even believed that bones could be used to tell the future.

This practice, called scapulimancy, goes all the way back to ancient Babylonia. People would heat bones over a fire and study the cracks and breaks. The pattern they formed became a map of sorts. Picture a treasure map made of bone but instead of it leading to treasure, it led to answers to specific questions.

Because of how important bones were to our ancestors, they were treated with great care after the rest of the body had decomposed. For example, some Native American peoples would place bodies on high platforms in the woods. After a long enough period had passed, they would go see how the body was doing. They would then carefully remove any rotting flesh that was left (ugh) and then preserve the bones for burial in sacred places. Once they picked a burial site, ancient cultures often placed important objects with the bones. They believed the dead needed not only their bones to travel the afterlife, but also things like money, art, and clothes. Even the bones of their pets were buried with some bodies.

Burying pets is an especially unusual choice because animals don't bury their dead; humans are the only ones who do. While some species (like elephants) might acknowledge death before moving on, humans are the only ones with rituals surrounding death, like funerals and memorials. Some animals even eat their dead to keep them from falling into the hands of predators. (Hope you weren't eating while reading this.)

So why have humans always gone through so much trouble to preserve the dead in cemeteries and burial grounds? Why do we place so much importance on the ritual of funerals and placing bodies in caskets to be lowered into the earth?

Besides cultural reasons, one answer crosses national and international barriers. Whatever remains of the dead, whether it's bones or a full body, is buried to keep the person from returning. To keep their spirit—or whatever is left after someone dies—from harming the living. There's a reason zombie and vampire stories are so popular. People are paranoid that the dead won't. Stay. Dead.

CHAPTER 9

Native Custom

When the British arrived in Savannah in 1733, they found it occupied by Creek Indians, mostly of the Yamacraw tribe. The Yamacraw thrived on the land their ancestors had long occupied. They believed it to be enchanted. They thought the land was full of the energy from their ancestors' spirits, with the living and the dead coexisting peacefully. Because of these beliefs, it was very important for the

Yamacraw to stay in the Savannah area. The bones of their ancestors were buried all across the city, allowing their ancestors' spirits to be available to them at any time. Moving away would decrease that connection and the energy that came with it.

For the Yamacraw, spirits inhabited all objects in their lives, both natural and man-made. They even believed that plant and animal spirits remained after death. They could seek guidance from everything around them. Because of this belief, they tried to live in harmony with nature and honor it in everything they did. Every action they took, and every part of their lives, had a deeper meaning. Their beliefs were the foundation for everything else.

The Yamacraw believed that the world was divided into three parts: the Upper World, the Lower World, and This World. By maintaining a balance between the supernatural realms of Upper and Lower, they believed they could ensure success and health in This World. The Upper World was inhabited by the creator that they called "The Master of Breath." The creator revealed to them rituals and prayers that kept the Upper World ordered and pure. Those who had a "proper" relationship with the creator received blessings and health.

This was the opposite of the Lower World, which was polluted and chaotic. Ominous, scary spirits lived there, as well as spirits of the dead who had not or could not make the final journey to the Upper World. It's hard to describe how much they feared the Lower World. Even among tribes who had similar beliefs, the Yamacraw were the most fearful of the Lower World and letting it become out of balance.

Basically, everything in their lives depended

on balance, both in the Upper and Lower Worlds and especially in their daily lives in This World. Men did men's work. Women did their own. Hunters did not farm. All functions had a purpose. This led to rituals to balance their own lives as well as the three worlds.

Here's a good way to try to understand. You probably know at least something about the laws that govern what we can and can't do. For example, if you speed while driving, a policeman gives you a ticket and you have to pay money. If you break the law, you're arrested. After you appear in court to answer for what you did, a judge or jury will decide your punishment.

The Yamacraw had their own system of laws. They wanted to make sure to quickly correct anything bad that happened to maintain the balance. And they believed the creator gave them the tools to correct any imbalances. By restoring balance in This World, they helped restore balance in the Upper and Lower Worlds.

But then white settlers came and changed everything. The different beliefs and customs of the settlers and the Yamacraw natives often collided with each other. This caused confusion, pain, and even violence. Because

both the Yamacraw and the settlers weren't familiar with one another's beliefs, they had a lot of trouble enforcing each side's laws.

The Yamacraw view of the three worlds is somewhat similar to how some religions and cultures view Heaven and Hell and God and the Devil. If you're "good" on Earth and live a balanced life, you might go to Heaven. If you're not, then you may go to Hell. Different societies over time have held similar but different beliefs and rituals. For example, the Greek and Roman versions of the Gods and the Underworld had the same figures and myths with different names and details. Other religions and cultures believe, like the Yamacraw, that their ancestors' spirits linger, providing guidance and protection. They have family shrines and leave offerings for their loved ones who have died.

What about your family? Do you have

any beliefs that are similar to the Yamacraw? Do you believe in a version of a "good place" and a "bad place"? Do you believe that family members you've lost have stuck around to help and guide you?

Founding Fathers
Part I

Every city was founded by someone. Savannah is no exception. General James Oglethorpe, who was mentioned earlier in our tales, laid the foundation for Savannah and the Georgia colony. But he wasn't the only one. Yamacraw Indian chief Tomochichi helped found the city. And as often happens with historical figures, each, in their own way, stirred up both controversy and loyalty during their lives—and after their deaths. So much so that the bones of these two great men became something of an issue in Savannah for years.

Remember reading about Wright Square in the tale of Alice Riley, the first person executed in Savannah? This same square is where Chief Tomochichi was buried in 1739 (only a few years after Alice). A large granite boulder allegedly marks his grave, but that's not the whole story.

There aren't any ghostly sightings of the chief to tell you about. But be careful! Legend has it that if you run around his burial rock three times and place your ears close to it, you can hear him calling out from the grave. Some also say that certain people, if they listen closely while walking in the square, can hear him speaking to them in his native language.

When the white settlers arrived in Savannah in 1733, the Native Indians of Tomochichi's tribe greeted them with a celebration. They hosted a large gathering on the Savannah Bluff. The Indians honored the newcomers with their finest clothing and dances that told the stories and sacred traditions of their tribe.

When Tomochichi and Oglethorpe met, the chief told Oglethorpe why his people had settled in the area. They did so not only for the area's position near a river and the ocean, but also because the tribe's ancestors were buried there. As you've already seen, the area would have had great spiritual and cultural significance to them as the resting place of their ancestors' bones. You also know they believed the spirits of their ancestors roamed the land, leaving an energy that protected and strengthened the tribe. To leave would be unthinkable for them.

Old maps detail an area marked "Indian Hill" in the historic district, which was part of the burial ground for the tribe. This burial mound no longer exists. It was destroyed sometime between the late 1750s and late 1770s. So what happened to all the bones? Supposedly, the bones were moved to Emmet Park. What we don't know is if all of them made it. But we *do* know that the resting place of many Native Americans was disturbed by the settlers to make way for the new city of Savannah.

I promised to tell you how Tomochichi's bones became controversial, and I haven't forgotten about that. You see, Tomochichi and Oglethorpe reportedly became good friends. The chief was said to be close to many of the British leaders in Savannah. Before he died in 1739, he told several people he wanted

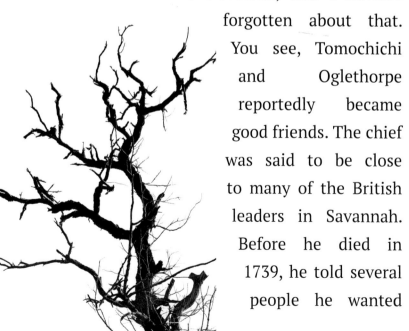

to be buried with his British friends. Whether that was his primary motive or he just wanted to be buried near his ancestors doesn't matter. Oglethorpe demanded that the chief be buried in the British style in Wright Square. He wanted the chief to have full honors, including soldiers shooting guns over the grave, a tradition still used today in military burials. As part of his burial, it's said the chief was buried with his blanket, headdress, and weapons.

Oglethorpe also insisted that the tomb be marked with an impressive monument to both the chief and his ancestors. An obelisk was placed there. An obelisk is a tall, pointed column rising from the ground. (You may have seen obelisks when reading about ancient Egypt, where they were common.)

Over time, as the tribe moved away, authorities wanted to ignore the Yamacraws' impact on the city of Savannah, so they removed the tomb from maps of the city. Sometime before 1871, the obelisk honoring Tomochichi was also removed, but no records can be found.

We do know that, in 1871, a beautiful garden mound was placed on the site in Wright Square. However, in 1882, the government removed it to build something to honor William Washington Gordon, who founded the first railroad in Savannah. Remember Willie Gordon, who loved his wife so much he came back from the dead to get her? Yep, that's him. But his daughter-in-law Eleanor did not want the monument to go forward without a new one for the chief. She did not want to disturb the resting place of Chief Tomochichi. And she was upset at how the history and traditions of the Yamacraw were being treated. She knew the importance of Indian burial grounds.

So they installed the large, granite stone that

marks the spot now. The city held a ceremony to honor the chief and recognize his assistance in establishing Georgia and Savannah. Judge Walter G. Charlton gave the speech honoring the chief, admitting that he didn't know where the chief's bones were, but it didn't matter. When dedicating the memorial, Charlton said that the chief was "all Georgia dust by now, and all Georgia is his grave."

It turns out, however, that the destruction of Tomochichi's burial place was probably just rumors. His grave appears to remain undisturbed in Wright Square, even if no one is exactly sure where it lies.

Founding Fathers
Part II

You know that James Oglethorpe founded Savannah and the Georgia colony. You know he was a friend to Chief Tomochichi and advocated for his inclusion as a founding father of Savannah. What you don't know is that Oglethorpe was the center of an international incident after his own death. The strange tale begins with a university.

To honor Oglethorpe's founding of Georgia, Dr. Thornwell Jacobs started Oglethorpe University in 1913. He established it in Atlanta, the capital of Georgia, about 250 miles from Savannah. Once it was up and running, he had another idea: move Oglethorpe's bones to rest right on campus. But there was a problem. You see, even though Oglethorpe founded Georgia and Savannah, he was British by birth. So when he died, his remains were buried in England, as were his wife's. He wasn't even on the same *continent* as Oglethorpe University.

Dr. Jacobs used his influence to get key people in the British government involved. But the government didn't have authority over the bones. Since Oglethorpe and his wife had been buried under All Saints Church in Cranham, England, the rector of the church was the only one who could release the bones. To complicate things even more, the old church had been demolished. When the new church was built, the markers that showed where all the remains were buried were taken down. No one knew exactly where the bones were located under the new building!

But that didn't stop Dr. Jacobs. He was on a mission. Both United States and British officials must have thought him ridiculous, but finally, he found proof that the foundation of the building had not changed. That meant that Oglethorpe would be exactly where he was originally buried. And Jacobs knew where that was from old documents. So, in 1923, stones were removed from the foundation of the church so Dr. Jacobs could get to Oglethorpe's crypt. Jacobs lowered himself into the crypt by a rope, like a graverobber! There he found his prize. But his fight wasn't over yet.

Initially, Dr. Jacobs had support from both the United States and the United Kingdom for bringing Oglethorpe to the university. But once the bones were found, officials in Savannah began to argue that the bones belonged in Savannah, which Oglethorpe founded, and not in Atlanta, where the university was. Making things even more complicated, the governor of Georgia got involved. He said Oglethorpe's remains should definitely come to Atlanta but rest in the state capital. It seems no one but Jacobs wanted the university to have the bones.

The British papers were especially harsh to Dr. Jacobs. They called him a body snatcher and accused him of robbing Oglethorpe's grave. But what did that really mean? Was body snatching something common? It actually was, but you'll have to check out the next chapter if you want to know more about that.

The outcry was so strong that Dr. Jacobs finally gave up. He withdrew his request to bring the bones to Georgia only six days after finding them. James Oglethorpe has stayed at rest under the church in Cranham, England, ever since.

Body Snatchers

With all the superstition and ritual surrounding burials, it's obvious that people throughout history care about their loved ones resting in peace. But it wasn't always meant to be.

In the late 1700s and early 1800s, doctors needed human bodies that they could carefully dissect and use to teach their students. But it was illegal in Georgia to dissect a dead body (until 1887). So doctors had to get and dispose of corpses in secret. Believe it or not, body snatching became a thriving business beginning in the early 1800s. Doctors often kept one person on staff full-time to get bodies, but they often needed more help. So anyone who had a shovel, a strong back, and the guts to sneak into cemeteries and dig up smelly dead bodies could make some money. Body snatchers, known sometimes as "resurrection men," stole as many as forty thousand bodies a year to sell to medical schools. You read that right, forty thousand!

How did they get away with it? They focused on fresh graves. Body snatchers worked in groups to carefully exhume—that's fancy for "dig up"—a body from the grave and then make it look like the grave hadn't been disturbed. They had a multistep process. First, they'd remove dirt at the head of the grave and put it onto a canvas sheet so no dirt would get on nearby graves. They'd pry the coffin lid open and strip the body of its clothing, leaving behind everything but the body and any valuable items like jewelry, which they would keep. Finally, they filled the grave back up with dirt, leaving it just as they found it.

Body snatching became such a problem that coffin makers began to change their practices. Coffins became harder to open. And more were made of metal because it was sturdier than wood.

While most snatchings happened in larger urban cities like New York, Baltimore, and Philadelphia, smaller cities like Savannah prepared for the worst. The wealthy began to build structures that would house and protect their loved ones.

We can see today that Savannah's older cemeteries like Colonial Park and Laurel Grove contain mostly crypts and family vaults to hold the dead. The structures are made out of stone bricks and contain entrances that are *buried underground*! That's how serious a problem it was. This prevented body snatchers from getting into the crypts. You had to travel down a set of stairs to get to new bodies, which were laid on shelves. More bodies would be added over time. When the crypt became crowded, the oldest bones would be relocated to a special box called an ossuary in the center of the room.

If you visit Savannah, make sure to take a stroll through one of its cemeteries to see the elaborate vaults that cover the crypts. The wealthy took great pride in designing the final resting places for their extended family.

Vaults are carved with family crests, angels, and poetry. Some of them look like famous buildings with classic architecture or appear to be more chapel than tomb. For many, the vaults became just as much a symbol of status as the home they lived in while alive.

Buried Alive

Remember how I told you Victorians were worried that people weren't really dead and could be buried alive? Well, that fear had long existed, and certain situations in the Victorian era made the paranoia even worse. So much so that it infected their culture and eventually changed how the dead were buried.

Many tales and legends throughout history deal with the dead coming back to life.

Even now, zombies and vampires freak us out, even if we don't believe one will actually come walking down the street. But during the 1700s and 1800s, medical science was still developing, and doctors admitted they couldn't always tell if someone was truly dead. To freak people out even more, there were actual cases where people who appeared dead—BUT WERE NOT— were buried alive.

Popular media at the time (books) heightened the paranoia. The publication of *Frankenstein* by Mary Shelley in 1818 led many people to question what it meant to be alive or dead. It featured a monster built by a scientist from spare body parts (probably snatched from graves). Once the parts are stitched together, the monster is brought to life by a spark. Is that enough to make it human?

Famous author Edgar Allen Poe's 1844 story "The Premature Burial" featured a woman who was placed in the family tomb. Three years later, when her husband opened it to place another (dead) family member inside, her bones fell into his arms. It seems she had escaped her coffin and then tried to break out of the tomb. She got stuck in the iron bars at the entrance and died standing up. That's the stuff of nightmares right there, and it made Victorians terrified it could happen to them. Being buried alive became a popular topic for pamphlets and newspapers, and many people and organizations took advantage. For example, in 1896, the London Association for the Prevention of Premature Burial was founded (really). They published written materials—at least seventeen—playing on the public's fears.

As the hysteria reached a breaking point, coffins were modified—again—so they could be opened from the inside. When a coffin was buried, ropes ran to the surface and attached to bells. If the person buried was alive, they could ring the bells and hope someone heard them. If they didn't, then they had to start digging and pull themselves out of the grave, covered in dirt.

You can picture it happening, can't you? Their hands breaking through the surface and clawing at the edges of the hole the coffin was placed in. Their faces pale as they gasp for breath. It would be like something out of a horror movie. And how would we know the person was really buried alive and not a zombie? If you saw someone climbing out of a grave, what would you think?

CHAPTER 14

Moon River

In these pages, we've encountered some of Savannah's haunted places, but we saved the best for last. The Moon River Brewing Company is a favorite of paranormal fanatics. This restaurant and brewery is still in operation today. This means you can grab a burger with a ghost *if* one decides you're worthy. The paranormal television shows have all filmed there, and countless people have encountered something supernatural when visiting. Unlike most haunted buildings, though, Moon River is home to both friendly and not-so-friendly ghosts.

The most popular friendly ghost is the one the staff refers to affectionately as Toby. Toby is about the size of a boy. This shadowy figure mostly sticks to the basement and doesn't generally bother anyone except for a push here and there.

Other ghosts roam the upper floors. Visitors and workers have heard footsteps and voices in vacant rooms. People often report being shoved by something invisible, especially on steps. They also report something invisible grabbing their clothing or their arms or legs. Mostly, people consider the ghosts at the brewing company a little pushy but not scary—although the ghosts *have* thrown bottles at visitors a few times and trapped some in the bathroom stalls.

But no one would call the "Lady in White" friendly. She lurks in the shadows of the upper floors of the building. She's the type of ghost you definitely don't want to encounter. She's both ominous and bitter, and she doesn't like her space being invaded. She has scared off several crews of workers trying to renovate the building. During one renovation attempt in the 1990s, she violently pushed the foreman's wife down the stairs.

Many staff and visitors have seen her. It seems that she's likely the ghost of a hotel worker who died in the late 1800s. No one knows the true identity of Toby or the Lady in White. Before becoming a brewery and restaurant, the building was home to a hospital and a hotel (not at the same time). Toby and the Lady in White could be anyone. But one of

Moon River's most famous ghosts is someone we can identify because he died right there in the building.

In 1832, Moon River Brewing Company was the City Hotel. It was a popular place for people to gather for a meal or to conduct business, even if they weren't guests staying at the hotel. Sadly, many tragic events took place there over the years, but one stands out.

James Stark was a guest at the hotel. He and a local physician, Phillip Minas, had a longstanding feud with each other. One day, they challenged each other to a duel. You've probably seen duels in movies or heard of the famous one between Alexander Hamilton and Aaron Burr (back in 1804). Duels were usually reserved for when someone had insulted someone else's honor. Wealthy men at the time considered that to be the worst thing ever. And if you refused a challenge to duel, you would be branded a coward. No one would accept you after that.

For a duel to take place, the folks involved would choose a neutral meeting spot and time. The men would each come with a friend—their "second"—to assist. Sometimes a crowd would gather to watch. The men would stand back to back, walk ten paces in opposite directions, and then turn and shoot. Whoever survived won the duel.

After some back and forth, Stark and Minas couldn't agree on anything. But Stark spread a rumor around town that they had agreed to a time and place for the duel. Stark and his second went, knowing Minas wouldn't show up. They then came back to Savannah and told everyone that Minas had backed out, making him look like a coward. This crossed a line, leaving Minas no choice but to respond.

Minas went to the City Hotel to confront Stark. In front of a room full of people, he whipped out his gun and fired before Stark could even react. Minas's single shot killed Stark instantly.

It's not 100 percent clear which room James Stark was in when he was shot. Different versions of the tale have different locations. But we do know it was on the main floor, and his ghost has not rested since. You will find his ghost on the main floor, or sometimes on the second floor, where he was staying at the time. It's a good idea to stay away from him, though. He had a temper while he was alive, and he's been known to show it now that he's dead. People claim to sense his anger, and he's shoved people on the stairs more than a few times. He also likes to move and throw things.

One thing's for sure: if you visit Moon River Brewing Company today, there's a good chance you'll get a glimpse into the spirit world. Whether the spirit will be friendly or not is anyone's guess.

The Walking Dead

Our tour through some of the haunted legends and superstitions of Savannah has come to an end. But there's so much more to the story. For every tale we've told, there are several more. Savannah is a place that feels a bit out of time, like you could turn the corner and be in the late 1700s or early 1800s. The prospect of a supernatural experience is almost a given. It practically hangs in the thick, humid air.

We've only scratched the surface. If you visit Savannah, you can walk in the footsteps of these tales. You can also choose from tons of excellent ghost tours that will get you up close and personal to the spirits who lurk in the squares and mansions. Some of the experiences are open to anyone curious about the supernatural. But certain tours should only be attempted by those who really like to be scared.

Run around Tomochichi's grave marker three times and listen for his whispers. While you're there, see if you can spot Alice Riley looking for her baby. Make sure to ask the staff at the Juliette Gordon Low Birthplace about their ghost sightings. You can end the day having dinner at Moon River Brewing Company and hope that one of the resident ghosts grabs your arm or gives you a little shove as you're walking the hallways.

Savannah waits for your visit. But don't let your guard down. Savannah's shadows are alive with secrets.

Jessa Dean writes spooky stories for kids and has been a ghostwriter for multiple authors who unfortunately don't write about ghosts. She lives in Houston with feline overlords who like to "help" with her work. Her day job in law proves that truth is stranger than fiction.

Check out some of the other Spooky America titles available now!

Spooky America was adapted from the creeptastic Haunted America series for adults. Haunted America explores historical haunts in cities and regions across America. Here's more from the original *Historic Haunts of Savannah* authors Michael Harris and Linda Sickler: